Mule Sense 101 (Fool's Knowledge)

By

Darris L. Martin

Mule Sense 101 (Fool's Knowledge)

Mule Sense 101 (Fool's Knowledge)

Printed in the United States of America

First Printing: January 2012

ISBN- 978-0-9833992-6-1

Mule Sense 101 (Fool's Knowledge)

Mule Sense 101 (Fool's Knowledge)

Mule Sense 101 (Fool's Knowledge)

Mule Sense 101 Rules
Don't waste the brains of workers
It is ok to let workers think
The customer is always right and so is the worker
Listen to your elders
Work if you want to eat
Never eliminate profit
Eliminating the customer eliminates the business
Don't use envy to set prices
Don't use assumptions to set higher prices
Don't set prices assuming Americans will pay anything
Base airline ticket prices on cost and not volume
Cheap airline tickets are not tickets for everyone to fly
Your phone still works!
Always keep the mule working
The mule is the valued asset and must come first
Houses are not mules. Houses are depreciable fixed assets
Don't buy a mule you cannot afford
Mules stay at home, they never walk off just to go visiting
If you take a mule across town and leave it, the mule will find its way home
A mule's life today is the same as it was 100 years ago
All advertisement does not work
You do not have to add advertisement revenue to everything
Everybody does not like your ads
A tired mule blocks out orders and stops listening
If only one mule uniquely made you rich, then that mule was used unethically
Look at the birds. They don't plant, harvest, or gather the harvest into barns, yet they eat. If you leave a mule along, he will also eat

Farm Work

Mule Sense 101 Rules
Don't waste the brains of workers
It is ok to let workers think

Mule Sense 101 (Fool's Knowledge)

I was raised in Mississippi. In fact right in the heart of the Delta. For everyone that knows nothing about Mississippi, it is famous for its rich farm land. The soil is most likely the richest you will find anywhere in the USA. It always has been that way and will most likely never be outdone in the future. The reason is simply the soil in the Mississippi Delta is fertile from hundreds of years of deposits by the Mississippi River. This river has a very powerful, fast moving current that carries deposits from the northernmost regions of the country all the way to the Gulf of Mexico. Several of those deposits collect along the banks as the water travels down river. And every now and then, there are floods that pick up the bottom of the river and move it onto dry land in the Mississippi Delta.

But I am not trying to write a book about the river. I just want you to understand the Mississippi Delta is famous for farming. So try to change as much as you like, but if you are raised in the Delta, you are exposed to farming. Now it was and still is possible to grow up in the area and not end up being a farmer, but you really have to work at avoiding that fate. I did exactly that. Even as a little supposed to know nothing boy, I knew I did not want to be a farmer and I had to do something to get as far away from the farm as possible. Now that does not mean that I totally missed being exposed to the occupation. If you were born in the area, you were exposed. Even the rich people were farm owners or otherwise connected to farming and servicing farming.

In my case, it was expected. So yes – I learned how to pick cotton (by hand), chop cotton, slop the hogs, feed the chickens and on and on. I never liked the work. But my grandmother was a farmer. In fact she was a big land owner and the only thing that kept her from having a very big farm was her getting too old to do the work. And that is where being a grandchild did not pay off for me. All of her grandchildren spent their summers working for her in the fields. I think she must have let other workers go just so she could put all us to work in the summer. I had cousins who were so ashamed of working all summer on a farm that they would lie to there friends and tell them they had spent their summer in places like New York City or Chicago. In actuality they were down on the farm.

It was hard work and my grandmother was a very hard task master. She taught us with an ironing cord as an incentive and she was very religiously strict. I was ok with the religion, but some of the rules were really out there. For instance, she said women (and young girls) were never supposed to wear pants. But if you ever worked in a cotton field, you know your legs would be scratched continuously if you did not wear pants. So grandmother's solution was to make the women and my teenage cousins wear a dress over the top of pants in the field. You can just image how hot that was in Mississippi in the middle of the summer in an open field with no shade at all.

When you really think about it, we were being treated the same as a farm work animal. You had no say in when you worked, how long you worked, what work you did, or how you did the work. And don't even dream about being paid. You were family and you were supposed to be happy that you could still get to eat and sleep in the house. Sleeping and eating in the house was no picnic. All you got for a bed was floor space and a quilt. One half of the quilt was your mattress and the other half was your cover. The house was not a five star hotel. I mean it still had an out house. For those who do not know what that means, the house did not have running water. So the bathroom toilet was a shack out behind the house in which you sat on top of boards built over a hole in the ground. There was no shower, but once a week, the tin bath tub was set up in the middle of one room. You had to go outside, get your own water and boil it to get it hot. Even when you washed dishes, you had to go outside to get the water.

Now getting water was real fun. My grandmother had big barrels around the outside of the house she used for catching rain water. But rain water was only used for cooking. All other water came from the pump. The pump was connected to a pipe that ran to the creek. How the nasty creek water got clean enough to use in the house, I never understood. But I remember many a time priming that pump to get the water to come out from the creek.

Well I think you understand when I say I really felt like a farm animal. In fact I felt like a mule. I could just sit all day and compare my life to the life of a mule; and since I did not have to use much of my brain to do this work, that is what I did most of the day. I could pick cotton from sun up to sun set and all at the same time list examples of how my life seemed just like the life of a mule. I was just another working animal on the farm. I had to get away from the farm.

One thing I learned very early in my life. If you spend enough time working on any problem (math, business, or even some life problem), you will eventually think of a solution. In fact that is the strength I have used all my life to become known as a problem solver in my career.

Now I was working on my first tough problem in life. It was, "How to get away from the farm?" It was the beginning of the summer. All the grandchildren were in their places working on the farm. I had to get off the farm. I had to go back home. Well I discovered by accident that if you rubbed a cotton stalk against a cut, you could easily infect the wound. And that is exactly what I did. I got a cotton stalk; brought it into the house one night of the second week on the farm that summer, and I rubbed it on my leg until I could see the blood. Then I rubbed that wound most of the night. By morning, it looked terrible. For sure, I needed to go see a doctor. I had developed some kind of rash. My grandmother summoned my parents. We went straight to the doctor and they concluded I had gotten a bad rash because I was allergic to something on the farm. So I was ordered by the doctor to stay away from the farm. Just like any smart mule, I knew how to get them to give me the day, no, the summer off.

The next year, my grandmother decided she was too old to farm and she started leasing out her farm land. So I never had to go back to the farm. That was my first mule sense lesson. I learned labor was just another resource no different from any other material used in industry. I learned a man working in the field is not different from a mule working in a field. A man working in a factory is just like a piece of raw steel in the same factory. We are just people mules.

Now I know you are sitting thinking you are not a mule. Well for many years now, industry and business in general have classified and used people as if they were mules. Today, a lot of money is being expended on processes to try to change this situation. But this is one situation that is very hard to change. Even with Six Sigma, lean manufacturing, and the empowerment of the team, we still have not eliminated the extensive processes that exist in our businesses that control every action of the workers – to the degree the workers can check their brains at the front door in the morning and pick them up again at the end of the day. They will not need them while at work.

We are just mules at work. Why do I say mules? Well looking back over my limited farm experience, the work of the mule was most likely the most brainless task I every saw on a farm. I mean, even the job of a dog could be improved to where they became watch dogs giving warnings of the approach of other animals (such as snakes, foxes, raccoons, etc.) that might harm farm animals. Even a farm cat or a barn owl would hunt small rodents and rid the farm of those animals. But a mule just ate, waited on the master, and let the master hitch him up so he could pull the plow all day. The mule never had to think. Yet, the mule always did have a brain and could think.

Years after finally getting away from farm work; after I had grown up working in my parent's dry cleaners, gone to college, and started my own career, I came to a shocking realization. My work in the real world was not very different from my work on the farm so many years ago. In fact when I made one of the few decisions they let entry level people make, I would fail to make the right decision when it was based on what I was taught in school. But when I based my decision on what I picked up from my limited farm life, it was a success. I remember as a young trainee being allowed to watch extremely high level corporate executives make a few decisions. I was shocked to learn they based their decisions on emotions, values they gained in their home life and just what most would call common sense. So when I tell people I am basing a decision on mule sense (my own form of common sense from the farms of Mississippi), it is not so out of place. When they considered the logic of the decision, I had little trouble convincing others I knew what I was talking about and my methods had merit.

In reality, it was not the method I selected to use but the common sense that made it work. It was not that I had discovered some incredible approach to business I call mule sense, but it was that I started using my brain. I started thinking. I used common sense. Since no one considers the use of common sense to be very novel, I called it mule sense.

Mule Sense 101 – Don't waste the brains of workers

Mule Sense 101 – It is ok to let workers think

Quality

Mule Sense 101 Rules
The customer is always right and so is the worker

Mule Sense 101 (Fool's Knowledge)

In the end everything about working with a mule in a field is positive. It does not seem that way at the time you are performing the work, but it really is. When you are plowing a row while following the mule and step into the mule's droppings because you did not see the droppings fall, you cannot see much that is positive. But in time those droppings will fertilize the soil and your foot stepping in them will help push the fertilizer into the ground. The same is true with what has taken place in Quality over the last three to four decades.

I have worked with and around the Quality organizations and operations of major corporations for more than twenty years. You learn a lot in time, but some of what you learn is not as positive as you would expect. One important thing I learned is there is really nothing new in that function of the business. Oh there are always people coming up with a better way to do things, but once you really understand the basic principles, those new and better ways turn out just being the flavor of the month. Let me try to explain.

Mule Sense 101 (Fool's Knowledge)

I have been a participant and developer of Quality initiatives under the following programs that at the time of their fame were considered to be the only way to do business.

- o Quality Circles
- o Quality is Free
- o Cost of Quality Improvement
- o Quality Improvement Teams
- o Statistical Process Control
- o Quality Improvement Program or Process
- o Total Quality Management
- o Quality Functional Deployment
- o Work Out Quality Improvement Program
- o Six Sigma
- o Utilization of Multiple Tool Set (i.e. Value Stream Mapping, Quality Functional Deployment, Six Sigma Design, Design of Experiments, etc.)
- o Lean Aircraft

Mule Sense 101 (Fool's Knowledge)

o   Lean Manufacturing

Most will dispute this statement, but all of these are just different flavors of the basic process of improving by encouraging improvement in the gemba. What is the gemba? It is a Japanese term that means workplace where day to day activities are performed. So all of these programs are designed first to create methods of getting workers to think and secondly to get the businesses to utilize the thinking of the workers. I know that is a great simplification. But I have been in this game a long time. I have yet to see something uniquely profound (to steal a term from Deming) about any of these approaches. Yes, each has unique process steps and each has its own specific utilization or application criteria, but they are actually not that different.

Let me break it down. A Quality Circle was a group of workers in one area of a factory who worked together to manage their own work area. As a practice, they accepted any and all responsibility management was willing to release to their authority. In fact, factories that released the entire responsibility for a work area had greater success with this approach than factories that limited the responsibility to trivial things like personnel absences and status reporting. These quality circles were later replaced by Quality Improvement Teams, with the only difference being the addition of management and leadership to the Quality Circle. Primarily the addition was only created because executive leadership was not comfortable with the delegation of responsibility to Quality Circles without managerial supervision. So Quality Improvement Teams did not really add anything new to the process. And guess what, the same was true with the addition of Total Quality Management, Six Sigma, and even Lean Manufacturing. Oh, there were and will always be some new rules or mandatory process steps, but those are just the reaction to the fear of losing control on the part of executive leadership. If you fear giving control to workers, then you create lots of process steps or rules that you think will limit the distribution of responsibility. Still the bottom line is the best process improvements will always come from the gemba. As long as you allow the gemba to do its job, you will sustain adequate improvement. And that improvement will be in the form of incremental improvements and quantum step improvements (which are generally associated with major process enhancements).

So that was my un-fancy way to build the case for "there is nothing new in the Quality Improvement world." Since time began, the goal has and should be to get the worker to think and to get leadership to listen to the worker's thinking and adjust accordingly. Such a simple concept is hard to implement. It is against human nature to implement any process where the boss has to listen to the leadership recommendations of the worker. Mankind's failure to accept this principle has been the primary limiter on the overall progress of mankind in this world. The most profound ideas are going to the grave with the people who create the ideas without anyone ever even knowing the ideas exist.

Mule Sense 101 (Fool's Knowledge)

It is sad when you stand back and look.

How could any one person think they have become so smart and so wise that they know more or better than every other worker in the industry, or in one business, or even in one factory? In most cases the leader in the factory did not get their job based on their knowledge, but rather on who they knew. So why do we think they become more knowledgeable one day after they start their leadership roles than someone under them who has spent a lifetime in the process?

What is wrong is we have let pride become the primary motivator of the common manager or leader. Their pride has become an attribute in today's industry that is even praised by other executives. Knowing deep down how foolishly those new leaders are performing, we entertain and even act on there nonsense proposals as if they will change the entire world. Well, knowing how to review and survey a customer's satisfaction or how to evaluate such responses is good, but it is far better to know how to pick up the phone, call the customer, and provide the customer with the service they really want, which makes them become satisfied customers (measuring satisfaction vs. creating satisfaction).

I would much rather have a team of people who can perform the developmental work required to solve design issues rather than the person who can make great presentation slides and develop outstanding milestone tracking processes to track the design issue and its resolution.

I would rather meet with someone who is going to tell me the truth about how bad things are rather than someone who is going to tell me whatever they think I want to hear to cover up the issues.

No matter how skillful you have become in relaying the status of a situation from your staff to me — your boss, I still would rather get the message straight from the mule's mouth. Why do I need you in the middle just to repeat the message and add cycle time to making effective decisions?

Mule Sense 101 (Fool's Knowledge)

Well this is not intended to be a Quality Management book. My intent is just to show the total lack of using common sense (mule sense) in the business world. To resolve the issue and bring about the fundamental change, we have implemented various Quality Improvement programs. All of these programs are designed to facilitate the use of the worker's common sense.

Mule Sense 101 – The customer is always right and so is the worker

So it is time to stop thinking leaders are the smartest and start thinking about listening to the worker. Consider a man, a mule, and a plow going down a row in a field. Who is the leader and who is the follower and what is just going along for the ride? The man thinks he is the leader, because he thinks he is the smartest. But if I remember correctly, the man follows the mule and the plow. No matter how smart the man may be, the mule is the leader and even the dumb plow that goes along for the ride is ahead of the man. Get use to it, the greatest leadership has always been done from behind. Ask any great Army General and he will tell you, young men go ahead to fight wars and old men (including Generals) stay behind to plan wars.

Banks

Mule Sense 101 Rules
Listen to your elders
Work if you want to eat
Never eliminate profit
Eliminating the customer eliminates the business

Mule Sense 101 (Fool's Knowledge)

Years ago banks were run by smart farmers and children of farmers who went off to colleges. That was because farming was the primary industry; thus farm money started the banking we have in this country today. As a result, there used to be a lot of people running banks who had mule sense. They grew up on a farm and they understood common sense. Their banking skill was a combination of what they learned in schools and their foundational knowledge from the farm. As time progressed in this country and we experienced the shift from the farm to the industrial revolution in the cities of the nation, the banking industry also shifted from the farmer's bank to the Wall Street's bank. The only problem today is that we are missing the people with mule sense in banks' executive leadership.

Why did the banks fail? Everyone knows it was poor management driven by the greed of the bank leaders. Well that is my take whether you agree or not. Some very smart businessmen were more interested in lining their own pockets with profits than they were with achieving the success of the banks. No matter how hard you try, you still can only be devoted to one task at a time. A mule knows this. That is why a mule plowing a field will stop to take a leak. The mule knows he will not be able to walk, take a leak, and not get it on his leg at the same time. The mule knows he can only fully be devoted or in concentration on one thing at a time. A mule knows this but people do not. They still think they can multi-task everything in the world. All they are really doing is giving a lot of attention to one item and overlooking the others. But the trick is to keep switching which task gets the most attention, so no one will notice your failure on any one task. I have a saying, if you try to be the best at doing everything well, you will end up doing very little well, and nothing best.

So the bankers wanted to be great at their jobs. But their desire to be even greater at making money took priority. It drove their decisions. It occupied their time and effort. It was more important than shareholder value.

Now don't blame the bankers. They were just doing what they had been taught to do. It is the training they obtained in school. It is not the training they got from the leaders before them. Most current leaders skipped on-the-job training. No one listens to the elders anywhere. Not in banks, not in business, not in government, and most of all not at home. In fact that is where it all went so wrong.

When these groups of leaders were growing up, they never listen to the adults. Instead they acted as if they ruled the world. And their parents let them get away with it. "It looks so cute. They are acting like adults. They are so smart." Well it was not smart. They were children and they needed to be taught to listen to elders and not to act like they knew more than their elders.

That little failure has created a group of leaders who think they know everything and who fail to listen to anybody.

You see this type in every walk of life. Think of all the Hollywood stars who have gone wild in the street because they stop listening to others and decided they were the only knowledgeable people in the world. Almost like little gods. They did what they wanted and expected everyone to agree with them. And if you did not agree, they did it anyway. Well a funny thing happens when an idiot takes over. We all start doing idiotic things. If you follow a mule with a plow and just let the mule lead the way, most of your rows will end up straight. But if you try to decide what is straight and pull on the rings to make the mule go in the path you consider straight, the rows will start being uneven and curved. Why? Well it is for two reasons. First, the mule is the elder. I know you think you are smarter than the mule. But most mules pulling plows did the work for years before the so called master behind them showed up in the field for the first time. Second, the mule has a better vision of the field than you. There is nothing in front of the mule to obstruct his vision. But the mule is in front of you and obstructs your vision.

Hey mister farmer, it is time you learn to lead from the back of the bus. Most of us think the best seat on a bus for driving or guiding a bus down the road is the front seat. That is why they put the driver's seat up front with all the tools for controlling the bus. But the best seat is actually in the back. I know you say you cannot even see the road from the back seat. That is true, but if you know how to drive from the back seat, you will be able to use the eyes of every passenger on the bus to help you see the road. Clearly, the man at the back has a greater opportunity to be the best performer because the man at the back has the power of every other performer to make himself the best.

The same is true in running a bank or for that matter a business or a family. You have to learn to use all the talent around you to obtain the greatest results. Just depending on your own skill is going to result in failure. To do that, you have to give up a little pride and listen to others.

You know the greatest political leaders of all times were the ones who learned to listen. Instead of starting meetings by declaring the answer before the question or with long statements of policy, they started meetings with an open opportunity for each advisor to make their case. They listened to conflicting views and they gave special consideration to minority opinions, i.e. the ones everybody else in the room wants to silence. Then based on the collective data, they made an informed decision. The only risk in the process was not having enough time to hear every opinion and having to intelligently stop the debate early and face the ever-present issue of making the wrong decision due to lack of information.

That is what the bankers failed to do and we suffer their failure. We paid our tax money to fix the problem, but we just now understand the repercussions of the bank failure. They just multiply as we continue to experience world crises after world crises. The old people use to say, "When it rains it pours." We have seen the Wall Street market and the housing market fall apart and neither is anywhere near recovery. In fact, they will not recover. We will just forget how good they used to be and become content with what they are.

All of this just because some parents who did not want to be like their parents failed to correct and teach their children to listen. I know you think I am over simplifying the problem. But I am not. Every big problem has a very simple, small beginning. Solutions only come by having the wisdom and knowledge to understand those simple beginnings and taking responsibility to correct those problems. Any great math genius is able to finally comprehend this principle. That is why, once they have found the solution to a major math computation, they always indicate it was so simple.

The same was true over the years in the development of various Quality Improvement models. You watched the development. There were Quality Circles, then Quality was determined to be first and reviewed compared to the cost of Un-Quality. Then we moved to Total Quality Management and Continuous Improvement. Along the way we worked with Quality Function Deployment, Six Sigma, Statistical Process Controls, Lean Manufacturing and several others. We created teams, focus groups, and the like that followed strict common process steps in solving any and all problems. And all that was great. But what was really going on was the simple application of common sense.

Some very smart person finally determined that people involved in the process are the best people for resolving the issues of the process. So each version of the Quality Improvement movement over the last several years was only designed to force us to get people involved in the process and start following a systematic process for the resolution of problems in their own area of expertise. The rest is just naming applications and very clever statistical tools of analysis. You could spend a lifetime in these applications and make it into several careers. But the whole thing is as simple as I noted in this paragraph.

So parents, before you decide to start making critical changes in the way your children are trained, take time to remember that no matter how much you hated the training you got as a child, it still made you who you are today. And if the world did not fall apart on your watch, maybe that training was not such a bad thing and maybe it is ok to use the same approach with your children.

Animals like horses have used the same methods they learned from there parents with their off spring for centuries. They seem to turn out ok. I mean, since the horses have not yet tried to revolt and take over the world from humans, maybe the old methods are ok. Even the ones your parents used.

Mule Sense 101 – Listen to your elders

So here we are and we do not seem to see an end to this madness. The banks failed. We taxpayers bailed them out at great expense. But why are we still feeling the pinch? Our homes are still being foreclosed. Our credit cards are being cancelled and our credit rating is so bad it is useless to look at that measure anymore. In fact, considering the number of people in trouble from a credit prospective, the use of that measure is losing its value. People and businesses have to be evaluated in other ways, since such a large percentage of them are in credit trouble. Besides that, there are too many people who specialize in making your credit record look good, even when it is actually bad. It is just an issue of knowing how the scores are calculated. So what now?

The banks are going to have to change. Right now, even under revised leadership in many cases, they are still missing the message. Have you ever wondered why the mule goes to work every day the farmer comes and gets him? You know the mule is bigger and stronger than the farmer. The mule could decide he has had enough any time, and very quickly end it all for the farmer. But that event rarely if ever happens. What makes the mule feel it is ok to continue to work in the fields?

Well it is simple, if you do not plant, you will not harvest. If you do not harvest, you will not eat. Even the mule has figured that out. He is not so dumb he does not know the connection between plowing the field and later eating the harvest. This is a basic principle of life. It applies to almost anything. You've got to work to eat. If you are not already wealthy and you never work, soon you will never eat. That is true for a person, but what does that have to do with a bank?

Mule Sense 101 – Work if you want to eat

The banks got in trouble and discovered they had made a lot of bad loan deals. They lent money to people and those people were beginning to have problems paying them back. Homes were foreclosed, lines of credit were terminated. The amount of credit available on almost everyone's account was reduced.

Simply spoken, credit got tight and banks stopped lending money. Well when I was in college studying and getting my finance degree, I remember being told banks make profits on loans. If you reduce or eliminate those loans, you also reduce or eliminate profits.

The home mortgages, the credit cards, and the lines of credit are the seeds of the bank that formulate the bank's loan crop. Banks plant the seeds by lending money. The harvest is the interest and fees they collect on those loans. When economic hard times hit and the banks took a slap for poor management, they curtailed the loans. Well that did improve the solvency of the banks, but it also cut off the profits. If the banks maintain those practices for much longer, they are going to start reporting major losses. So now the banks are sitting on property that cannot be sold, because no one can qualify for loans to buy the property. Well if you foreclose on existing customers and refuse to lend to new customers, how long will it be before you are out of the business. That is exactly what is going to happen if the banks keep saying no to loan deals they used to approve without discussion. People with perfect credit and lots of money do not need to borrow money. Only people who lack money and have minimal credit ratings need money. The mule that stayed in the barn all day does not need a rub down at the end of the day. It is just the mule that worked in the hot sun in the field all day that needs the rub down. People with great money profiles (good credit ratings and high amounts of collateral) do not need to borrow money; they already have money. So you have to set the lending rules so you will be able to lend to people with poorer money profiles (lower credit ratings and little collateral).

It is my guess that several bank leaders were replaced by shareholders right after the bank failures. But it is also my guess that several of the new leaders will eventually lose their positions for lack of profits due to the new rules on loan approvals.

Mule Sense 101 – Never eliminate profit

So what to do? It seems like everything ends in more disaster. Well there is a better approach. Instead of foreclosures, terminations, and credit limit reductions, banks should have tried to restructure loans and council clients. Instead of forcing clients into bankruptcy, they should have forced them into conferences with loan officers and pushed restructuring. In a restructure you get something. In a foreclosure you just get a piece of property, which loses value and cannot be re-sold easily. And now with the legal problem related to ownership, who knows when you will even be able to attempt a resale. All of this time the bank is just losing money and fueling even more home value loss in the housing market. I think it is far better to take a few extra years to get a profit rather than fixing everything so everyone has to take losses for the next few years.

Mule Sense 101 – Eliminating the customer eliminates the business

Who will fix this mess? Maybe no one can fix it. All I can say is I am thankful my house is still worth more than I owe. No one knows how long that will remain the case. But I am forced to keep the house because banks will not lend anyone the amount of money needed to buy the house even at the reduced value. And people who already have enough money to buy it without loans don't need a house. My house is becoming a mule put out of a job by a tractor, and is only good for the glue factory.

So what is the chance we will ever get a new set of bank executive leaders that have mule sense. Who knows? We may never get those types of leaders. That leadership club is a very closed and private club. Most of the controllers of that club do not have mule sense, so they are unlikely to select new leaders with mule sense. But one thing is for sure, the current bank executives will all be changed. They are on a path that assures there removal by shareholders. I wonder what we will get next.

Pricing

Mule Sense 101 Rules
Don't use envy to set prices
Don't use assumptions to set higher prices
Don't set prices assuming Americans will pay anything

Mule Sense 101 (Fool's Knowledge)

How much does a mule cost? I wonder how to set the price for a mule. Most likely mules are sold at different times in their lives. Some are sold at birth, others after they have grown up and have become farm workers, and yet others when they are good for nothing other than glue. But the price of the mule is most likely based on what value the mule will offer to the prospective owner. And maybe part of the price is also based on what the mule cost the seller. Now I do not know what that value or cost is, but I do know what it is not. You see, the price of the mule has nothing to do with how much I envy, desire or covet the mules my neighbor owns. The price of the mule also has nothing to do with a bunch of assumptions I made up and convinced everyone that the world runs on my assumptions. And most importantly, the price of the mule has nothing to do with how much you think I will pay for the mule.

So why did everything get so expensive? The prices of gas, food, electricity, cars, and almost anything you name. All the prices went up and do not seem to have a cap in sight. I think two things are working in the background. Most people just call it inflation. But inflation does not just happen by coincidence. Something or somebody has to incite the run on prices. So what or who did it?

I know you are thinking, why this fool would think he knows what or who drives world prices. If he knows so much, then why is he not out running the world? If the world was run by people who really understood what transpired, then they would have put a stop to at least half this stuff going on today before it happened. If you knew what was wrong, no one would be able to shut you up. You would scream it all day or until somebody listen to you. Well I do not know and I do not understand. I just have a few mule sense comments to make. Maybe one or two of them will cause you to laugh. If not, maybe they will make you feel better about the mess we are in.

The primary reason prices go up is envy or greed. I cannot stand to think you are better than me. So if I make a little more profit; then I am better. I will raise my prices just a little so I will make more than you. You think that view is shocking, well think about this. The primary reason prices go down is also envy and greed. I cannot stand to see you get more customers than me and (I assume) make more money than me. So I will drop my prices just a little so I can steal your customers and make more than you. You know if you plow a field with two mules side by side, you will have to use a dual yoke to keep one mule from out running the other mule. People are the same way. Two neighbors claim there is no envy or greed between them, but human nature tells a different story every time. Two workers doing the same job side by side will naturally start competing with each other. That's why if you want a teamwork spirit in the work place, the first thing you need to do is to make sure each member of the team has a different role in the workplace. Envy or greed is very powerful. It kicks in even when we are not thinking about it. And the drive is so strong in our society that it is even taught to students in school. Since students are trained to compete against each other in school, did you expect it to stop once they were in the work place? Now a lot of managers would say they want competitive spirit in their workers. That is true as long as that competition is directed to your marketing competitor. But when it is turned on fellow employees of the same company to the degree it causes internal destruction, or worst when workers turn it on you the manager, then it is time for it to go away.

Mule Sense 101 – Don't use envy or greed to set prices

Let me show you an example of envy or greed setting prices. I purchased a brand new home and moved into the home at the beginning of the winter. That following summer I turned on the air conditioning units for the first time. There are two units in the house. One of the units blew up immediately. Since this was the first time the unit had been turned on, it was fair to assume it was installed incorrectly. So I called the original installer. His first words to me were "The labor warranty period is over." I had not even asked him to come and fix the unit. I was just explaining what happened and this guy was already positioning himself not to correct his mistake for free. Well I did not complain. I just asked him to come out, look at the unit and let me know what needed to be done and how much it would cost. He came out. He told me the compressor blew up. He said he could fix it; the parts are covered by warranty but his labor is not. But since he knew he made an error in the installation, he would only charge me half the normal price of his labor. When I got the bill, half his labor cost was $120.00 an hour. Now I have not been away from the cotton fields so long that I did not know that price was a lie. I mean, many executives in major corporations don't make that much an hour. That works out to be almost $250,000 per year on a 40 hour work week for an air conditioning repair man only charging half his normal labor rate. What would make an air conditioning repair man demand such a price? Nothing could do it but envy or greed. He wanted the same thing he saw the executives getting, so his price went up to get it. I assumed he doubled his normal price so he would force me to pay the full labor cost. I assumed correctly. I have had the same guy do other work and the $120.00 per hour is not half of his labor cost. It is his real full labor price. Sometimes I really hate living in the state of New Jersey. Envy and greed are so bad here.

Mule Sense 101 (Fool's Knowledge)

Let me show you some examples of how prices have been driven by this envy or greed. Some people (those in the food industry) think you and I will pay the price of food no matter how much it increases. They think you've got to eat. Since it is a basic function and everyone has to perform it to live, then you cannot stop buying if the price gets higher. Sellers think buying habits for this type of item are unresponsive to increases in prices. Wrong! There is no such thing as a product that is unresponsive to increases in prices. All buying is responsive to increases in prices. It took the consumer a little while to learn how to respond to the continuous increases in the prices of food items. But the consumer now knows how to respond.

Here is what happened. Initially, the only alternative seemed to be to continue paying the higher and higher prices. But I talked with a lot of consumers and they began to change where they shopped for food. I remember telling one lady, "I have not seen you recently at the neighborhood super market." She responded, "I stopped shopping there. I now only buy food at one of the local one-dollar chain stores." Now I had been in those stores previously and as I remembered they had very little area for food. They sold other stuff. But have you been in one recently? They are expanding the food area to almost half the store. Why? They have lower prices and people are flocking to their stores to buy any food items available in their stores. Those stores have changed enough in the past twelve months to be able to facilitate all your super market shopping needs.

And they are not the only ones. All the other low-priced stores did the same. It used to be that only the poorer people in a community went to those stores. But check out the parking lot. The cars in those lots today are clearly increasing in value. Rich people are feeling the pinch and now shopping at the discount stores. So the revenue of the super markets dropped! You can tell it did because they are selectively reducing the prices of some items to unrealistic (for them) prices. The items with price reductions are items that are commonly carried in the discount stores. For example, most two litter soft drinks are $1 or less in discount stores (all brands). In many super markets they have marked down the soft drink aisle. They offer most brands for $1 and some off brand names for less. Only a few brands have prices of as high as $1.50. But gone forever are the $2 and $3 prices for two litters of any soft drink. And that is just one item. You will also notice an increase in the number of places the super markets are stocking discounted priced items (for instance, the new all items for $1 aisle). What happened is the consumer learned how to force price reduction. Now if the super markets and the discount stores don't start learning the basic mule sense truth about prices, they will over adjust and end up selling items under cost due to consumer pressure. Continuing those practices will result in losses and business failures.

The same thing is true in other related industries. For example the pharmacies are beginning to feel the pinch. For some time they were the only trusted places for several non-prescription items. But now the discount stores are taking that business. The discount stores have expanded their selection and cannot seem to keep their shelves stocked, while the major pharmacies are having problems selling items before they exceed their shelf life. In addition, the pharmacy is also hard hit by the Internet pharmacy (both legal and illegal). Today prescription drugs may be purchased legally via the Internet from any country that offers drugs at discount prices under their laws. And unfortunately, the illegal market offers the same drugs without prescriptions, cutting out both the high-priced US pharmacies and the high-priced doctor visits required to obtain prescriptions. Keep in mind, people will not pay any price for medication.

Mule Sense 101 – Don't use assumptions to set higher prices

What about automotive gas? I can remember in my lifetime, paying less than thirty cent a gallon for automotive gas. And that amount included the state taxes. The only tax assessed by most states for the purchase of gasoline used to be sales taxes. These days, if they just removed the tax from the price of gas, we would not even complain about the base price inflation experienced over the years. I use to buy all my gas from Indians on their reservation or at least the property they claimed was their reservation (which included almost one-third of upper New York State.) Don't start thinking that is foolishness. Even the courts agreed the land belonged to the Indians. Well the Indians do not pay any federal, state or local taxes. So they could sell the gas at cost plus profits. But all the area businessmen got together and begged them to charge higher prices so they would not put the non-Indian stations out of business. Well they agreed and only reduced the price to about 10% below the competition. Then the Indians proceeded to buy up every service station in an entire county of New York. But even a 10% cut, while it was less than the taxes included in the price of gas at other stations, was still worth an out-of-the-way drive to buy cheaper gasoline.

So what happened to gas prices? Remember the gas wars … when one station on one corner would reduce their price just a hair below the competition that was located right across the street and put out a big sign to attract all the customers. If you asked them a question about it, they would tell you their brand was more efficient and therefore offered a better price. In reality, the gas they sold on one side of the street usually came for the same refinery as the gas on the other side of street regardless of the brand. The blend (additives) may be different, but the basic gas and the cost of purchasing the oil and refining the gas is the same for both stations regardless of brand. So everything else about the price is pure envy and greed; which started the gas war and never left it. In fact if you look closely at the prices of different stations in the same general area, you will still see price wars going on, the same as ever. But the difference in the prices is very small. And no one is doing a lot of advertising price differences since it will only put a brighter light on the real problem of all of the gas prices being too high. Now it is hard to guess when to expect price increases. They are no longer tied to cost. It can be anyone in the distribution chain that decides, I am envious and it is time for me to be greedy and make more money. Sometimes, I think they take turns in who will be the bad guy today. One thing for sure, people in the chain will not tell you who upped the price. They do not want you to come down on anyone in the chain since it may be any of them next time. So every since price wars began, it was determined the public would pay almost any price for gas, whether there is a real shortage, a group slowing down production to jack up the price, a distributor holding reserves to force price increases, or just someone wanting to make more money. Anyone in the distribution chain can increase prices for any reason. That is why it is so hard to track specific price increases to specific disasters and world events.

Nobody knows the real connection because the price changes due to envy and greed have hidden all the realities of the market. With these small changes we experienced oil corporations growing overnight into the largest, most profitable corporations ever seen since the days that anti-trust cases broke up the larger oil corporations. And I do mean most profitable corporations in the world. As the change in gas prices was world wide, so was the overnight windfall profit growth. That is real good return for the little guy on the corner who used to have the grease monkey job that everyone looked down upon, now being the executive that sits on the top of Wall Street. And just think it is all because he believes you are willing to pay anything at that pump.

Is there an alternative? How do we as a country get out of this fix? It is very simple as usual. If I had a mule and could not afford to feed the mule, then I have two choices. One is to sell the mule and do without. But if I depend on the mule to plow the field, selling is not an option. The other option is to grow the food I need to feed the mule.

The same is true for your car. One option is to get rid of the car and you will not have to buy gas for the car. Now most of us will say that is not possible. But think again, that may be your best option. It will mean, using public transportation or walking. Yes, public transportation is available. How do you think your maid got to your house? After all, she came from the other side of the town. You should try it. It is not that bad. Now that also means, you will make fewer unnecessary trips. It will make you stay closer to home while you are not working. And finally, it will cause you to walk to a few places and probably lose and average of 10 to 20 pounds of excess weight within a year. Well I see no down side.

The other alternative would be to make your own fuel. Well we will not be able to do that to power our cars. But we can plan to park them more often. Just think how much gas you would not need if you cut driving down by 20%. A 20% reduction would not interfere with your work schedule; it would just eliminate the fun stuff.

Mule Sense 101 – Don't set prices assuming Americans will pay anything

The next time you try to sell me a mule, make sure you do not base the price on envy, greed, assumptions, or what you think I will pay. I am smarter than that even if I don't tell you how smart I am.

Airline Tickets

Mule Sense 101 Rules
Base airline ticket prices on cost and not volume
Cheap airline tickets are not tickets for everyone to fly
Your phone still works!

Mule Sense 101 (Fool's Knowledge)

What happened in the airline industry to ticket prices? Many years ago while the prices were regulated, they were fairly stable and the airline ticket price variance from airline to airline was not significant. But in case you have not noticed, it is now hard to find two people on the same plane with tickets from the same airline that paid the same price for the tickets. There are just too many reasons for ticket price deviations. Sometimes I wonder if anyone really knows how much it costs to fly a plane load of people to the next stop. I wonder if you divide the true cost of flying between two cities by the number of people that check in on the flight, would you find anybody on that plane who paid their fair share of the cost?

Well there are a few things going on in this pricing foolishness. First of all, if an airline is going to make money, then flying planes with passengers that did not pay enough for tickets to cover the cost of the plane will only lead to the eventual failure of the airline. If you do not believe me, check the history of failed airlines. Therefore, any marketing pricing approach that does not recover the cost of the flight plus profit should be replaced by a plan to dissolve the airline. And you have to deal with your true cost. There are some airlines that have been formed on a model of reduced cost (common planes to reduce maintenance cost, more short-haul smaller plane schedules, non frills, one class of seats, etc.) that can really fly from A to B for less. If you are one of those airlines, then use the lower cost. If you are not, use the higher cost. Pretending to be a low cost airline by setting aside a portion of your airline fleet to be low cost does not reduce the true cost of the flight very much since you still have overhead allocation and general and administrative costs to add to the set aside to get to true cost. In other words, an accounting shell game does not reduce cost.

And why are airlines reducing the price below true cost. Well the assumption is they will attract more customers and get a larger share of the market. Well a larger share of a losing market just results in bigger losses and going out of business sooner. You assigned a problem to a marketing guy to get more people to fly your airline and they came up with the solution. They reduced the price (for a complicated host of reasons). So now every Tom, Dick, and Harry can afford to fly. The prices are low enough to compete with trains and buses. In fact, the airline ticket price changes have created an entirely new market of cheap bus ticket companies that work on ticket volume without the overhead of bus stations and ticket counters just so they can compete with the airlines. Air travel has become crowded and air security has become dangerous because every class of people can now afford to travel by air. The next time you miss a flight because some guy in front of you did not know how to clear security, remember the marketing plan was to increase the volume of flyers.

Did you know the highest priced tickets on most flights are mostly purchased by the business traveler? That is for three reasons. First, the business supporting this traveler probably sells products and services to the airline. Therefore it is good business to put more cash in the hands of the airlines. Second, most businesses do not have time to shop around for tickets. In fact, most of the time they buy tickets on very short notices due to the great number of changes in business schedules. Finally, big business is most likely the only entity that can afford to pay full fare. If everyone else had to pay full fare, they would stop flying.

Now that is a novel idea. Do we really need to fly as frequently as we fly today? For years, mankind lived without all this travel. I mean, a phone call or even a letter was good enough years ago. What changed? Was it the needs of the world or the desires of the people in the world?

Mule Sense 101 – Base airline ticket prices on cost and not volume

Now some of you are thinking I am running the risk of denying free competition. No I am not. I am just properly defining competition. Some very poor MBA graduate decided free competition was the ability to set prices (such as airline prices) without the constraint of controlling laws; in a sense, setting the prices based on what the market would allow. Such a definition of free competition has become the way airlines compete for the lowest or highest prices. That is all great competitive spirit, but it overlooks the true field of competition, which is cost. Henry Ford was able to reduce the price of a car to an amount the average man could afford because he found a way to reduce the cost of manufacturing the car. He established manufacturing assembly lines which incrementally reduced the cost of manufacturing cars. Henry did not just lower the price without regard to cost. Henry also did not reduce his prices just to become more competitive.

The same should have been true with the airlines. Something should have been done to reduce the cost before the ticket prices were cut. Now in the case of some (low cost airlines) that was done. But the majority of the airlines just cut ticket prices without any basis related to cost. I think every airline steward understood the need to keep prices in excess of cost. Just think how many lost their jobs due to the smart leadership decision to cut prices to increase volume.

So how do we fix the mess? It is simple. Reset the airline ticket prices based upon cost. Make the ticket prices standard so multiple passengers pay the same price. Well you think you will lose volume and go out of business. That's right, you will lose volume initially. But your competition will join you in higher prices very soon. If they don't, you will eat their lunch because they will go out of business soon. Remember it is better to keep the plane on the ground than to send it up at a loss.

And what happens to the traveler. Well that is the one who really needs to adjust. If you cannot afford the luxury of air travel, then stay at home or do like most of us are learning to do and travel by car again. Get a low dollar gas burner and drive the long haul. You used to do it and maybe it is time to try it again.

I know it is hard to go back to old ways once you have enjoyed a little luxury. But sometimes you have to do it. When tractors appeared to be replacing horse and mule drawn plows in the fields, it was hard to hitch up the mule once you had enjoyed riding the tractor. But for many it had to be done. You see companies used to lease the use of tractors because farmers did not have the money to buy the equipment. So the farmer might lease a tractor just for the plowing season. But once the season was over, if he needed to plow a small area he had to hitch up the mule. Some of us need to hitch up our mules and start driving the long trips as opposed to flying. And if you cannot drive, then it does not mean you have to get on a plane. You can still travel by train or by bus. Traveling by bus almost sounds like ancient times. But it is still done today. If you ever take the time to drive on a long trip again, you will notice how many people are still traveling by bus.

Mule Sense 101 – Cheap airline tickets are not tickets for everyone to fly

Don't fly works for businesses just as it works for individuals. Years ago, we did business around the world and never left home. In those days it had to be a real emergency to put an employee on a plane. Usually only the owner or the chief officer would make a trip for the company. Today, every Tom, Dick, and Harry travels for the company, to the extent that one of the conditions of employment with several corporations is your willingness to travel. Travel is communicated in percents. You know the job involves 30% or 50% travel meaning you are on the road traveling 30% or 50% of the time. Well years ago we knew how to pick up the phone and conduct business. That option is still available today. You just need to become trained again on the use of the phone as a business communication tool. Now do not fall into the trap of trying to get too fancy. For instance, many will tell you to conduct video conferences over secured networks or even over unsecured computer networks. Well those are nice, but expensive, especially when they are private, secured networks. And let's be truthful, most of our business is not really

private.   Don't confuse your desire to be secretive with a true
need to be private.   The number one reason for privacy in
business today is not security, but secrecy. You just do not want
anyone to know what you are doing.

A plan simple phone call or conference call will do the trick
most of the time. I have experienced some of the biggest projects
I have ever worked being done totally by phone. It only takes the
willing commitment of the parties to work by phone.

Mule Sense 101 – Your phone still works!

Bottom line, you can stop or greatly reduce air travel. Just try
it. Set a reduction goal and make it work. You will not see any
reduction in business volume or business efficiency.

A man has two farms. One is in upstate New York and the
other is in Mississippi. His primary crop in New York is apples
and his primary crop in Mississippi is cotton. Both farms use the
services of mules from time to time. In Mississippi, they are used
to till the soil, plow for planting and even plow to thin out the
field. In New York, once the trees are grown, the mule is a work
animal hauling empty baskets to the field and bringing them back
full of apples. Now if one of the mules dies, the farmer would
not put the remaining mule on a travel schedule flying him back
and forward between the two farms to get all the work done.

That would be expensive and foolish. Just buy another mule or rent one. You may even be able to borrow one temporarily. Likewise, if the farmer lost a worker that plows with the mule in Mississippi but still has the worker that drives the mule in New York, he would not put the remaining worker on a travel plan to split his time between the two farms. That would be expensive and foolish. Just get another worker or lease one (temporary employee). So tell me again. Why do business executives decide to put their workers on travel plans today?

Housing

Mule Sense 101 Rules
Always keep the mule working
The mule is the valued asset and must come first
Houses are not mules. Houses are depreciable fixed assets

Mule Sense 101 (Fool's Knowledge)

The country is in the midst of a major transition of the typical housing trend for the average family. It is a big transition. Other transitions have happened in the past, although for the most part they were always in a favorable direction, with the exception of the Great Depression era. But today we are re-visiting issues similar to those experienced during the Great Depression. Fortunately some financial safeguards are in place to assure things do not get as bad as they have been before.

This country started with housing that was built around the farming community life that most residents enjoyed during the earlier years of the country. There were towns, but for the most part the towns were small because they depended on the farming industry to make them survive. Then the industrial revolution came and created the great factory towns. The farmers transitioned to those towns, which became cities. Housing went from the farm house in the middle of nowhere to the cheap (generally rented) space in the fast growing industrial or factory cities. This was the first major housing transition in this country. It went smoothly because most people were improving their living status. Even the families that initially rented in the cities were soon able to start buying and building in small sections of those cities. Some of the houses they built still exist until today. Now over the years there were many other elements (such as the depression, the start and end of wars, and new industrial locations selectively based upon the availability of resources) that caused additional transitions. The one major negative transition was the depression. Interestingly, that was a time more of homelessness than a time of family movement.

Today we are experiencing another great negative family housing movement. The loss of jobs and tightening of loan money are causing several people to lose there homes due to inability to maintain the mortgage payments. These factors have festered and resulted in a major increase in the number of homes on the market. Many of those homes are foreclosures. So a large percentage of the houses on the market today are owned and being sold by banks and similar financial institutions. Since banks and financial institutions are losing money on these deals, it has deflated the price of the homes on the market. Well that just backfired on everybody in the country. All at once and it does not seem to ever want to stop, our property started to lose its value. Without home owners doing anything that would deflate the value of their homes, the bottom fell out and the values dropped 15% to 60% in the last three years. The worst fear is the values may just continue dropping.

It is not fun to suddenly learn that your house is worth less than you paid for it. In fact, we are now in the situation of having people owe more money on their house than their home is worth. Then if you have to sell that home for any reason, you are in trouble. Even if you do not sell and even if you do not owe a penny on the house, you are still losing net worth at a rate that is faster than you can get raises in your pay to make it up. Everybody is losing value. For some, it has just become easier to walk away from the home rather than continue paying outrageous mortgage payments for something that is no longer worth the value of the mortgage. In most cases walking away involves bankruptcy or foreclosure.

For many years bankruptcy was unpopular and embarrassing. Not any more. Today it is considered your Government given privilege. People are going bankrupt and starting to rent. That is the housing transition. People are moving out of mini mansions into rental property. In this time of slipping values, renting may be the only way to avoid losing your shirt. At least when you are renting and the value of the property goes down; you can move to a more expensive rental property or just enjoy a lower rental price where you are currently living.

Now a few things are not moving with the market and must be addressed real soon. Property taxes are still assessed at the higher values of the homes. Insurance rates are also set at the higher values. Those and other similar elements associated with these homes need to drop in price. In my mind I would even say homes that lost their value should be receiving lawn care at lower prices today. Since all of those associated prices were growing as the value of homes grew, then it is now time for them to reverse too.

So what is really going on? Well I think you already know my view. This is another major bank error. Unfortunately, the approach the banks implemented to resolve the issues is just making matters worst. Personally, I see no end without someone regulating a portion of the banking business. What portion? It is simple, it is time for a bill to regulate mortgages until the housing market values are stabilized or improved.

If you were lending money to a farmer and he got in trouble and could not make his required payments, you could come in, take the farm, shut it down, and put it up for sale at a low price for a quick turn. But we all know that is just what the banks did and it did not work. It just reduced the value on all the other farms and put them into the same trouble the first farm had. In addition it put the primary function of farming in jeopardy. That primary function of farming was and is to provide food for the public. When all the farmers are in trouble, no one is providing food for the public.

Well if the first farmer had a mule, the last thing you want to do as you try to resolve the issue is stop the mule from working. When the mule stops working, everybody loses. You got to keep the mule working everyday in the field if you expect to have any chance of ever resolving the issue. So taking the first farmer's farm is the worst thing you could do to resolve the issue. Once you take his land, the mule has no place to stay at night and no food to eat. Soon no one will be able to get that mule in the field again and everybody will lose the only real value added asset on the farm. Now you know I am not really talking about mules. I am really talking about the American worker. You know the income earner in the home. Whatever you do to resolve this current housing crisis, you have to keep that worker in the field. We cannot afford to start losing the productivity of the worker. And the last thing in world you want to do is upset those workers so much they refuse to every go back to the field. I mean once you lose the American dream of being married, owning a home with two cars and at least two kids, why work? It is so easy to give up and go on welfare. The only true difference in a family on welfare and one off welfare is pride. That is why getting women living in a project married is always good. The women have no shame and will sit at home on welfare, but the men have too much pride for that type of life. Getting the women married brings the pride back into the home.

Mule Sense 101 – Always keep the mule working

Mule Sense 101 (Fool's Knowledge)

Even if I jumped all over the place on this topic, I still think you got the gist of the issue. But, let me see if I can provide some real constructive mule sense assistance.

- o Stop taking homes. Set a 30 to 90 day moratorium on foreclosures, bank seizures, etc. It would also be great if mortgage companies allowed customers to pay the interest and escrow for the next 30 to 90 days without principal. Put the principal on the back end of the mortgage loan (yes for a fee) just to give the consumer a break. Years ago, banks used to offer this type of service to help people with things like Christmas shopping. All of these changes would help keep the mule (the worker) housed under a roof.

- o We need a program of job creation. It may not ever be the great corporate jobs everybody used to have, but when this country came out of the depression, it did so by creating jobs (remember the new deal). Just build something whether it is needed or not to create massive numbers of jobs. Maybe they will be laborer jobs, but they will be jobs. I don't know, maybe it is time to rebuild the roads across America. That would put jobs in every community. That is far better than spending the money on another war or welfare program. This will keep the mule working. When the mule works, there is a paycheck and bills get paid.

o   Stop the bank's right to approve the terms of home sales. Clearly they do not know what they are doing. This is a job most of us have learned to leave to the real estate professionals.   That is who I use to determine good deals. It is not law, but going into a home sale without the direction of a Realtor is foolishness. Pass a law that forces the bank to buy in on a deal when it is negotiated between competitive Realtors for involved parties.   Otherwise, the banks will continue to set real estate prices erroneously. This will help the mule that is caught in the ditch get out and get back to work.

o   Force banks to stop lumping mortgages together and selling them to multiple stockholders as shares of stock. You cannot allow the whims of the American stock market to start setting housing policy, where the goal is just to make more money. Housing policy goals should simply be to assure adequate housing at reasonable prices to the most Americans. Housing policy should have nothing to do with making money on mortgages or from real estate price inflation. Two or more men owning the same mule will forever

disagree and fight about using the mule. There is no
disagreement when a single man owns a single mule.
There are other things that must be done, but this list will start
things moving in the right direction.

Mule Sense 101 – The mule is the valued asset and must come first

Our method of determining the value of homes needs to
change. I purchased a new home less than six years ago. At the
time of purchase, the home was listed on the market at $530,000.
Now that was considerably above my purchasing power. But it
turned out that the independent builder of this new home was
about to experience an increase in his interest rate, from the low
rate he experienced as a builder to the rate the bank expected if
the home construction was late or if the builder failed to sell the
home. So this builder decided to eliminate the windfall profit he
had built into his asking price and reduced the price to $430,000.
And I just happen to look at the house the day he dropped the
price. Well I jumped right on that deal and made an offer
assuming I was buying a $530,000 house for $430,000. Wow,
what a deal!

Fast forward to now (six years later). I just got an offer to
sell this same home at the maximum the market would allow,

which is $345,000. Yes, that is an intangible book loss of $185,000 or 35% in less than six years. That is an actual dollar out-of-my-pocket loss of $85,000 or 20%. A house is anticipated to have a life of somewhere around 50 years. Many homes have actually lasted more than 100 years when maintained properly. The banks and mortgage companies established their lending business on the basis that homes will maintain enough of their value to last at least 30 years (the basis of 30 year mortgages). So why do we have a system that will allow a home to loose 20% or more of its value (using any assessment method you like) in less than six years. Something is wrong with this system.

The opposite should also be true. Remember when the prices of homes were running away? There is something wrong with a system that will allow the value of a home to increase 20% or more in less than six years. Some foolish people are treating homes (which are fixed assets) as if they were stocks, bonds, or commodities. Houses are not stocks. The value system for houses cannot be the same type of value system you use on the stock market. One is a paper representation of future and present business potential. The other is a fixed asset. It is not intangible. Rather it is very much tangible.

The value of a house should be estimated in a manner similar to the way we estimate a piece of factory equipment. It has a value based on its actual construction cost and normal profit that should be depreciated over time. And yes, I did not say depreciated over time. Fixed assets do not increase in value over time. To think they do is simple foolishness. And any smart accountant would force you to book any value you think your assets appreciated into an intangible goodwill account instead of an account that values the equipment. The equipment will forever be worth its original first cost less depreciation. Now you can invest in improving that asset and add value to its first cost. But you cannot sit around and turn stupid dreams of greed into higher asset values on the books. And you also cannot just wake up one morning and decide the asset is overpriced and just reduce its value on the books. That is why the accountant gave you a goodwill account. Keep all your foolish dreams of greed and their variations in the goodwill account.

When the stock market went south, jobs disappeared, banks started to fail, major corporations started to fail, and the economy we used to love fell apart. Housing prices should have remained unchanged. The volume of sales, the number of houses on the market, and amount of new construction should have changed with the economy. Those things are always affected by the economy. But the price of housing should have been unaffected. Houses are fixed assets. They should just depreciate normally. In short, houses had nothing to do with the foolishness of mankind that led to and sustains the woes of the economy.

Mule Sense 101 (Fool's Knowledge)

How do you fix the problem? Well one thing for sure, it is a mess and most of the mess is not repairable. Some people are still walking around believing real estate will regain it higher pricing. It will never happen. No one who now knows they can buy a house for less will ever agree to pay the higher prices again. Houses are not stocks. When the world only allowed houses to gain value, everyone accepted the system. But now we have learned that houses can loose value; no one will ever again accept any system of houses gaining value. So the fix for the housing market is a permanent value/price reduction. The lower prices are here to stay. Everyone must lose money. Even the man that never intends to put a home on the market. His home is automatically devalued by the changes in the market around his house. It is worth less and you just loss the difference (realized or unrealized). So what needs to take place to stop the price reductions is a change in the method of valuing houses. It has to be changed by law. The law does not need to set prices. The law simply has to provide the method to freeze and baseline housing values/prices based on their market value today.

For example the initial pricing could be based on the assessed value of the homes for tax purposes. Using this approach accomplishes two important tasks. One, it will provide an instant increase in the value of most homes to something closer to what the owners paid for the homes. Second, it will give local

66

government a little insurance that everyone will not come in all at once and demand updated assessments that are more in line with values realized in today's market. Most communities are sitting on that time bomb that will cause the bankruptcy of the local government. This approach will eliminate most of that treat. And the good news is if someone is not pleased with the change in the value of their home, they already have the methods in place to appeal the assignment of value based on the tax assessed value.

This change in housing valuation will also improve the reality of all financial collateral. Today, that collateral has very little value due to the fast and continuous decline in the market value of homes. Collateral that was worth $500,000 six years ago is worth about $350,000 on the average today. So if you secured a $400,000 loan with this collateral six years ago, then the note is under secured today. In fact, the owner of the collateral is in a position where it is more financially prudent to walk away from the debt than to pay more than the collateral is worth.

After establishing new values for homes as depreciable fixed assets, then the accounting rules for the treatment of houses as fixed property to be depreciated on some schedule identified in the law should be set in place by public law. When that is done (a simple law and a simple change in accounting rules) the housing market will stabilize very quickly. The great advantage of this approach is that it can be performed by each local government. They have the tax jurisdiction and the most knowledge for accomplishing the task. And a community can make these changes independent of other communities. So no one has to pass state and federal laws to fix our housing problem.

Mule Sense 101 – Houses are not mules. Houses are depreciable fixed assets

Cars

Mule Sense 101 Rules
Don't buy a mule you cannot afford
Mules stay at home, they never walk off just to go visiting
If you take a mule across town and leave it, the mule will find its way home

Mule Sense 101 (Fool's Knowledge)

Why not just start with the conclusion so no one is held in suspense? Cars are far too expensive. In fact that is why someone came up with the method of leasing. It spreads the cost of purchasing a car across more than one owner or buyer, so in a sense it allows multiple sequential ownerships to pay off the bank's original investment. That is also why the banks started financing cars for longer than the traditional three years. Now five or six years seem more appropriate. Everybody just overlooked the old depreciation issue that was previously used to justify the three years and began acting like a car will last as long as the current loan or lease/loan periods will last. In reality, the true value of the car depreciates much faster and if the banks ever have to repossess the car, they will find that the car has less value than the remaining balance of the loan or lease.

Well there it is again, the banks are messing with the economy by trying to make more money and causing issues that will hurt this country for more years than the banks will last themselves. I did not try to write a book that picks on banks, but most mule sense leads in that direction.

So what to do, what to do? Simple, reduce the price of cars. It can be done. You just have to reduce the profit the industry is currently enjoying per car. And yes, industry will still make a profit. It just will not be able to pay those big executive salaries and those plush union contract clauses. Big executives will have to become like the rest of us.

A smart rich man pays no more for the care and comfort of his mule than a poor man. There is just no value in paying more. The rich man may buy a more expensive car, but his maintenance cost is about the same as the maintenance cost of the poor man. The poor man may skip his maintenance because he does not have the money, but the needs of the two cars are basically the same. That is because two mules, one rich and expensive and one poor and cheap cost about the same to maintain. They eat about the same amount of food and need about the same amount of barn space.

But how did cars get to be so expensive in the first place? I think the greatest increase in the price of cars was caused by the high utilization of leases. Prior to leases, everyone was concerned about the price of a car. The public monitored prices from year to year. Car makers worked hard to keep the year-to-year same model price increases below $500. I would be afraid to make that comparison today. With a lease, no one is concerned with the overall price of the car. They just want to know how much they must pay up front and how much they must pay monthly. Then, they will investigate the mileage limits and residual value that can be rolled to the next lease. The dealer, bank, and car maker could be doubling the price of the car. As long as it does not increase the monthly lease fee, who cares? And that is where the problem began. Now the prices on those cars have reached a level so high that no one other than the very rich can afford to buy a new car. In many cases you cannot get the car financed over enough years to make the payments reasonable. And all this increase in price happened with no one complaining because no one noticed. Today you almost cannot find even the cheapest new car of any size for less than $10,000. I remember when that was enough money to buy a luxury car. Not any more!

So what has happen to America and cars? Well most people still have enough income to afford lease prices. They are therefore driving new cars all the time that never exceed three years in age. They have no plans to ever buy a car. If something happened and they had to buy a car, they would never be able to afford it. They will have to buy one of the cars coming back off a lease and it will have almost no value the next time they needed to trade. In fact, if you fall off the lease wagon, you will most likely start the oldest car habit of poor people. That is driving cars that are in excess of ten years in age. By the way, many of these cars run great but may not look so great.

Mule Sense 101 – Don't buy a mule you cannot afford

Mule Sense 101 (Fool's Knowledge)

Well all of this sounds good and interesting, but what we really need to hear are some real practical methods to get out of this hole or to survive while in this hole. You know when a mule falls into a ditch and cannot climb out of the ditch the way it got into the ditch; there is always the possibility of just walking in the ditch until you reach a place where the sides of the ditch are not too high to climb out of the ditch.

1. America needs to get off the lease trail because that trail will only lead to failure. Sure you seem to be able to afford a more expensive car, but one day you have to wake up to the reality you really cannot. And when you wake up, you may find you cannot afford any kind of new car because the prices are inflated beyond your range.

2. Car makers need to get the price of cars down. Cut salaries, cut labor, close factories, get rid of those great union contract clauses and whatever else it takes. Make sure the pain is evenly spread between workers and management, but it is time to roll back the cost and price.

3. Failure to reduce prices will only end in low volume sales. You will start seeing a year-to-year drop in the number of new cars sold. Why? Simply because

people will start buying used cars and hanging onto their current cars much longer.

4. I heard a financial advisor say if you do not have the price of a car in cash in the bank, you have no business buying the car. You should not finance the car because you cannot afford the car. Well that is harsh, but I will add something even harsher. You also cannot afford to lease that car if you cannot afford to buy that car.

5. This country needs to once again start investing in alternate methods of transportation. Better city and town bus service would help. Perhaps this has never worked before because it was always designed to fit massive needs. Well it can also be designed to accommodate smaller needs. For example, airports run small buses or vans between terminals. That is a cheaper approach than the expensive trains. A similar approach is used for poorer hotel workers in places like Atlantic City. They call it the Jiffy. It only costs a few coins, only travels up and down one street (by all the casinos and hotels), is always over crowded, and runs frequently enough for you to disregard the schedule because the longest wait for the next ride is only about ten minutes.

6. Investing in improved city transportation will aid the economy, environment, city budgets, comfort, and pleasure of the people. People would prefer hearing politicians discuss transportation improvements rather than more service cuts to balance budgets. While such improvements will cost in the near term, they will add much needed jobs immediately. Thus in the long term these improvements will also add revenue and reduce cost.

Now there is one more mule sense comment related to cars. This comment is hard to accept because it impacts our daily lives. Simply put, **STAY AT HOME**. This country continues year after year to increase the amount of traveling it does across the town, the country, and the world. Years ago, if a kid wanted to play soccer, he went down the street and played with his five or six friends in his own community. But today we have the soccer moms and dads who drive their kids half way across the state and spend a night in a hotel with the entire family just to allow one child to play a two-hour soccer game. Think of the cost for gas, food, lodging, and your total loss of rest the entire weekend. After a restless soccer weekend, you are happy to go back to your normal job. It is so much more peaceful. And what good is all this doing for the kids. Your child is not a good player. In fact, maybe these kids do not even like the game. Hey they are never going to buy you a house out of their check from playing professional soccer. And if you think they are growing from the experience, you should get out of your hotel room and check out the real environment of the hotel community that you are exposing your child to week after week. Those low priced hotels you stay in are also the primary cheap hotels used by cheating husbands and wives. And that is who your child talks to when you let them walk around the hotel lobby for a while. Before you know it they will have all the secret codes down. You know the rooms with the cracked open doors, the pools and saunas with low traffic and no oversight, the lobby bars, rest rooms, and phone banks. Once one has spent a few years as a road warrior as I have done, you come to know these places of inappropriate opportunities. I mean you are staying in a house of bedrooms. What do you think goes on in those bedrooms?

Years ago, the school, church, work, restaurant, and anything else we enjoyed were almost within walking distance. If we had to drive, it was not very far. In fact if someone asked us to go somewhere that required more than ten to twenty minutes of driving time, we would have to plan the trip and schedule the date well in advance. But now many people commute hours each way, everyday just to go to work. So getting into a car and driving two hours just to sit in a restaurant and have Sunday dinner is not considered unusual or extreme. Well the time has arrived for us to come back home and stay at home a little more often.

Like most things that have gotten out of hand, you have to re-train yourself to live without those things you now consider customary, because they are really just luxuries. Consider phones. I remember when there was only one phone in the house. In fact some homes did not even have a phone. I remember people coming to our home just to borrow the phone. Or even better, I remember getting calls and having to run next door to get the person who was being called. But today, every six year old has a private cell phone. And who are they calling or texting? What could be so important at that age? And they are really using those cell phones. Just look at your monthly bill and you will know that is true. It is not really needed. The world and they will survive just find without all those phones. You know recently I started a habit of breaking my cell phone use. I put the phone down and stopped carrying it everywhere. It took a little while, but now everyone knows I may not answer if they call. And texting, I stopped that long ago. If you want to text me, send me an email. I talk on my phones. Oh I know how to text with the best, I just also know I do not need to text. Texting does not rule my life. I also do not use my phone as a computer. If I need to get on the Internet, I use the computer and not the phone.

Keep it up America and before you know it, they will have you making love to your husband or wife on a cell phone. Just put the cell phone down. At least turn it off every now and then. Years ago, we used to turn them off when we went to sleep. Today the only time young people turn them off is when they accidentally run the battery down.

Stay at home. You do not have to do everything. You do not have to participate in everything. Your favorite team can still win a game if you are not in the stands. You are not the life of the party and those foolish parties will go on with or without you. You may want to believe it all evolves around you, but it does not. It was here before you. It is doing fine while you are here. And it will go on long after you are gone.

Stay at home. One of the biggest drivers behind broken marriages and broken families is failure to communicate. It is not that families no longer know how or want to talk; it is that they no longer have time to talk. Because you are away from home so much, you may be spending more time with an office colleague than you are with your own mate or child. So no wonder out-of-marriage and out-of-family relationships develop. You are just falling for the one you spend the most time around. Go home and stay a while. Marriages and family relationships require effort to maintain. You have to put in the time. If you do not plan to put in the time, then get out and never go back into that type of relationship. You are better off renting or living in a hotel since you will never be home to fulfill your responsibility.

Stay at home. Add up the time you are at home in a week and the time you are away from home. Compare the two. If you are spending significantly more time away from home, perhaps you should question why you even have a home. You do not use it. Homes are very expensive. You are never there. You never entertain at home. You don't receive guests at home because you are not there when guests would visit. So why have the expense.

Try this simple plan to change your habits. While you are at home, turn your cell phone off. If someone really needs you, they can call you on the land line you haven't used in the last six months. Oh, they have the number. Come, come, if they really want to find the number they can. You are still listed in the old system called a phone directory. Then make your car off limits for a day or two at a time for anything other than going to work. Walk every other place you go. If it is too far, stay at home. Don't worry, you will surly not die and the world will surly not stop.

Mule Sense 101 – Mules stay at home, they never walk off just to go visiting

Mule Sense 101 – If you take a mule across town and leave it, the mule will find its way home

Now my advice to stay home is designed to save you money. Specifically, it is designed to reduce your dependence on a car. But as you can see, there are numerous other benefits.

Advertisement

Mule Sense 101 Rules
A mule's life today is the same as it was 100 years ago
All advertisement does not work
You do not have to add advertising revenue to everything
Everybody does not like your ads
A tired mule blocks out orders and stops listening

Mule Sense 101 (Fool's Knowledge)

The number one creator of issues today is advertising. It has really become an outstanding industry, if you are in the right position. But for those–which include most of us at one time or another–who are in the wrong position, advertising is the single most evil force we have face in life. And every time we face off with an advertisement, we lose. It is so intrusive that I have taken steps in life to reduce my contact with advertisements. My problem is the more I try to avoid advertisements, the more they seek me out by using new schemes. I have even found myself giving in to the ultimate sin of buying some advertisement time for my own business ventures.

I know you never heard anyone talk about advertisements this way but this is the way mule sense works. It is like getting kicked in the head by a mule. You know the mule is likely to kick. Yet you stand at the perfect angle to get kicked and tell yourself it will not happen to you. That is the story of an advertisement. A simple television advertisement is designed to get you to make a purchase. You know it in advance. You know the advertisement has been successful in the past. Yet you sit there watching the advertisement while saying to yourself, "It will not get to me. It will not make me want to go and buy something." And even after this mule kicks his hind legs into the air and aims for your head, you are still saying you will not get kicked. Well surprise, you will be kicked. You will eventually make a purchase. That is what the advertisement is designed to make happen.

When media like the television, radio, magazines, and even newspapers were originally conceived, the desire was to improve communication, news, and entertainment. But once again, some very smart persons (this time it may not have been bankers) decided they had found an outstanding method to pay the cost of all those modes of publishing and broadcasting. They decided companies would pay the cost of operating the media and an extremely nice profit to themselves just for the opportunity of putting a brief advertisement in the media along with the communication, news, and entertainment. It was planed to be a very small thing. You know three to five minutes between thirty-minute television programs, or one advertisement per newspaper print page, or two or three pages in a 30-page magazine. Just a small thing priced to pay the bills so that the real communication, news, or entertainment content could be freely continued.   Well that may have been the humble beginning, but the result today is that advertising allows some communication, news, and entertainment just to give advertising an ounce of creditability. In fact, today there are whole advertising programs called info-commercials.   Worst yet, there are entire television channels devoted to continuous advertisements (TV shopping channels). In a typical thirty-minute entertainment show, there are three to five-minute ads preceding the show, five minutes into the show, 15 minutes into the show, five minutes before the show is over and at the end of the show. When added together, half of the 30 minute program is devoted to advertisement. That is not advertisement to pay the bills on the part of the provider of the show. That is pure and simple greed to get rich at its best. In a daily newspaper, you now have multiple ads where each ad occupies two or more pages of the paper. That is on top of the fact that the other pages already contain more ads than communication, news, and entertainment. And we all know it. In fact we now pay premiums to watch television stations (premium movies channels) that exclude advertising breaks. We pay for radio stations (satellite radio) that do not advertise. We donate to pay for commercial-free educational radio and TV (even those programs have a number of "advertisements" referred to as corporate contributors or sponsors). What is shocking is that the premium cost is not high compared to the amounts companies pay for advertisements. If our premium amounts are enough to pay the bills for a television station, then what are they doing with all that extra money they are getting from selling advertisements? It must be profits in their pockets. What is up with that?

No one cares to change this system because everyone is just making too much money off the process. The advertiser is getting you to buy things you do not need by making you look and feel cool. The television station is getting you to keep watching the station longer and longer while getting less and less entertainment per hour watched due to increased advertising. The people who create the advertisements are making millions. Even the actors in the advertisements are making so much money that already-famous actors are signing up to create advertising media because it is quick, big money. A whole host of new program coordinator jobs exists just to make sure all of the commercials play on time and at the right cut-in for local commercials as opposed to having national commercials take place. A whole new marketing force was put into place just to go make money selling ads. And if that was not enough, the advertising fever has spread from television, newspapers, magazines, and radio to everything else. I have to wait an extra thirty or more seconds for all the ads to load on my computer every time I change Internet screens. In fact, the ads take up more than half my Internet displayed screen. If I do a search, the result is over fifty percent of advertisement, none of which I want to see. Worst than that, the advertisements are complicated and fail to load on my computer or lock up my computer because they require special software. Not to worry, there is always a small advertisement somewhere on the page for buying the needed software. If we responded to ten percent of the advertisements we see in one day, we would not have time to do anything else. We would also be broke and have the world's most junky residences, filled with all that worthless stuff.

Yes it is really intense. So intense that there are now companies that will sell you software kits that enable you to sell other people's goods online (like e-books), all without ever owning or handling what you are selling. It is like making money off the idea of selling something to make money without ever selling anything. The only product being sold is an advertisement. It is legal because that is what the seller promised to sell to you.

Advertising is way out of control and there is nobody out there that is going to get it back in control. If this keeps up, we as a nation and a world will defeat ourselves. I can only image what will happen if any of this junk gets into court. It will take half a century just to figure out who sold what to whom.

And people are going broke over responding to advertisements. I know you are thinking, just stop buying. But can you do that in today's world. If I do not get one of the new phones, won't I find in a very short period of time that I can no longer communicate with others because my equipment is outdated. You say it will never happen. Well let me give you some examples, just to inform you that it is already happening. Can you watch television on your old analog TV? Does your old rotary phone work in your new house? Can you find a 45rpm record in any store and play it on your old stereo? Do you even know where you can buy a cassette tape player? Soon you will not be able to buy VCR tapes. If you had a manual can opener, would you know how to use it? The world moves on and if you decide to stop participating in buying all the foolishness products, you will be totally out of touch in the twinkling of an eye. The last time I moved (less than six years ago), I had to buy all new televisions because the ones I had were not designed to connect with current satellite TV equipment. My sets were not that old and they all worked just fine. They just all had the wrong adapters. Now you say how did they work in the previous residence? Simple, I had the old connector boxes from the cable companies in the old house. Once I returned those, I could only get the new incompatible connector boxes. Sometimes I wish things would stay the same or at least slow down, but they will not.

One of the biggest drivers in this economy is the ever fast-changing and improving world, which forces many people into bankruptcy. Yes it will drive you into bankruptcy. It costs more and more everyday to keep afloat in this world. There really is no option to drop out. If you still think there is an option, ask some retired, elderly couple how they are managing expenses on a fixed income as they face continued cost increases. Oh it was fun when you could figure more and more ways to keep making more and more money, but once you are off the workforce track you are finished. That is why so many older people are resorting to some form of senior assisted living. They give everything they have to such businesses known to be overpriced, which causes older people to lose everything and become totally dependent upon the fate of the assist living institute. And the institute takes the risk that the old person will not live long enough to start costing more than the old person invested. The institutions are wrong sometimes, but on the average, they are right more times than they are wrong. As a result they make a good profit.

Mule Sense 101 – A mule's life today is the same as it was 100 years ago

So what is the real problem? The basic theory of advertising is the problem. It was started to help someone sell something of value. Today it has become the thing of value itself. Let me try again. The business of advertising has become more important than the products it is selling. In fact advertising has become so important, that it frequently is the only product. That sounds weird, but it is true.

I have a need to sell books. I am not good enough to have some big publishing company pay me a signing bonus and send me royalty checks monthly. So I have to figure out how to advertise and sell my own books. One method is using search sites on the Internet. You put together a short ad, maybe with a picture of the book and one sentence of text. The search company flashes the ad every time someone does a search using key words you selected. Then if that person sees your ad and clicks on the ad, you pay a fee for the click. The fee can be any amount from pennies to 10 or 15 dollars a click depending on the popularity of the search engine. If it only cost a few pennies, then rest assured that no one is using that search engine. So although you pay for someone clicking on your site, you still have no guarantee of a sale. In fact, all you are paying for is the opportunity to do more advertising. When the person clicks, you have to show them something that will make them buy the book or you have a cost and no sale. This is a case where an advertisement is used to buy time for more advertising. So the only real product for the clicks is more advertising. Do you want to know how well it works? Remember what I said earlier about doing a search on a computer and getting a page of results of which half are advertisements of things I do not want. So you learn how infrequently one buys from any of those ads. I mean do you know anyone who buys what's flashing unrequested on a computer screen. Even if one were interested in the product, most shoppers are smart enough to then deliberately look around on the web for other potentially better deals. Most likely the one with the most unrequested advertisement is not the best deal.

So just think about all that advertising money being expended for clicks or for flat-rate page displays that never ever result in a sale. Maybe somebody is getting business from the ads, but not me. I have yet to be able to trace a single click to the sale of a book. I think the only people making money on these advertisements are the people selling the idea that this is a way to make money.

Mule Sense 101 – All advertisement does not work

Computer advertisements have done one thing very well. They have slowed down computer processing. The ads are so complicated that they take too long to load. So you are sitting there waiting for the ad to load so that you can continue performing your desired functions. Now you cannot get rid of the ads. The owners of the websites will tell you the ads are paying for your privilege to use the sites. You get free email because you accept the advertisements. You get free credit tracking because you look at all the advertisements for more credit. You get free spam stoppage because you advertise the stoppage software every time you send an email. Everyday somebody is generating another clever way of pretending to give you something for free just so they can increase their advertising visibility. If you wish to use the free service, then you have to contend with the ads. I generally find there is always a paid service out there that performs the same task for a fee. So if you do not want the ad, you have to pay. If you want commercial free TV, then sign up for pay stations. If you want commercial free radio, then sign up for satellite stations. If you want computer pages that are free of advertisements, then only use paid services loaded directly on your computer.

For years, a farmer went out and purchased a mule to perform farm work. Today, if a farmer were still using a mule, most likely the farmer would never purchase the mule. In fact many farmers today no longer purchase farm equipment. Instead they lease the equipment. It is cheaper than buying equipment and seeing it depreciate and fall apart before you feel you've gotten your value from the equipment. Now smart lessees have started making money from advertisements too. So the truck or the tractor you lease will be covered with advertisement signs that may be seen from the road by passing drivers. Those advertisements are becoming a second income to the lessees.

What am I saying? If you were leasing a mule today, the mule would come with a sign on its back. Everywhere that mule went he would be generating advertising revenue. I wonder how long it will be before they figure out how to put advertisements on the skin of human mules?

Mule Sense 101 – You do not have to add advertising revenue to everything

Mule Sense 101 – Everybody does not like your ads

Ok. Since advertising seems to be here to stay, would it not be nice if advertisements were designed to stay out of the way. Smart advertisements, browsers, and search engines managers need to become sensitive to the customer desires and come up with advertisement that is a little more user friendly. Things like the following need to be considered.

o   On/off advertisement switches

o   A way to stop downloads and video buffered loading of advertisements with extensive video, or at least limit such advertisement to trailers on other existing video.

o   Come up with methods to avoid multiple advertisements at every level of clicking. For example, if you wanted to check out a news item, you initially get an advertisement as soon as you connect to the news service. Then you get other ads if you click on any specific headline. If the news report is video, you get an advertisement trailer before the news report and several trailer advertisements afterwards. Then the cycle restarts automatically with the next news headline even if you don't click on the next headline. The only way to stop the mess is to exit the web page.

o A method to only display video advertisements when users are displaying video content. Otherwise, the time required to load will depress the user.

o Consider advertisements that fade away after the user has been on the page for a specific period of time. This will allow users to stop being distracted by advertisements after being on a web page for little while.

So my recommendation is to curtail the expansion of advertising before the customer rebels and starts taking actions that will fully eliminate the capability of advertising, such as using paid programs that do not sell to advertisers or actually investing in software that will shield or block advertisements.

Mule Sense 101 – A tired mule blocks out orders and stops listening

Making It Legal

Mule Sense 101 Rules
If only one mule uniquely made you rich, then that mule was used unethically

Did you know that ethnical approaches to making money rarely result in making people rich? People who went from rags to riches usually did not do it with a normal eight-to-five job. Rather they were able to find something that was illegal in everybody's mind and make it legal. While that does not make your actions illegal, it does make your actions unethical. It is like taking a page out of a gangster's life story and using it in a very respectable legal business.

There are many examples of this concept in today's world. Just look at this list for a few we see in the news from time to time.

- o Companies that go overseas for the purpose of being allowed to hire workers at slave labor rates and working conditions.
- o Companies that create separate companies to conduct business that is illegal or unethical such as
    - o A major bank owning a check cashing service because of the unethical fees they can charge for cashing a check (a service performed by the major bank for free)
    - o A major bank owning a payroll loan company or a small loan company because of the unethically higher interest rates they can charge the poor

- Companies that start up new manufacturing businesses in foreign countries to sell their product and unethically get around import/export laws and fees.
- Companies that create International branches for the purpose of avoiding taxes in specific nations.
- Companies that create products that imply values that are not real values such as
  - Some vitamin producers/distributors
  - Internet business opportunities such as selling marketing to the public for a cheap fee without a real service
  - Law firms offering to reduce debt by negotiation, but are only inducing customers to default on debt for a large fee (this same service is offered ethically at no charge by several legitimate agencies)

This list goes on and on. Once you think you have seen all of the scams and cons, you will see a new one that you have never seen before. That is because everyday, someone else is trying to find a way to become rich without working. The American dream that used to be a dream of a free environment for living and working honestly has turned into an experiment in how to get rich quickly by ripping people off. There are countless examples in our environment. Here are two that are very unethical and yet extremely acceptable as legal.

For many years, there were two ways to borrow money in this country. One was very legal and very acceptable publicly. It involved going to a bank or similar institution and applying for a loan. The only problem with this legal method was most people did not qualify for a loan. When my parents built their first home by remodeling an old, three-room (shotgun) house, they were not able to get credit at a bank. Bank loans were just not possible for people of our status. Yet the interest rate on such loans was normal (just a small amount above the prime rate). The financial institutions making these loans made a normal profit on the loans.

But like most good things in the world, there is always a side that is not so good. A group of non financial institutions decided they could lend money to all the people who did not qualify for financial institution loans. Initially, these were gangsters that were looking for ways to put their illegally obtained money to work making more money. You see, the gangster could not take his money to the bank and invest it in certificates of deposit. I mean that really did not make sense, since in many cases the gangster originally stole the money from the bank. So the gangster started lending his money to the poor, but at high interest rates. They were called loan sharks. They were crooks. The interest rates started as high as 20% each month and could quickly accumulate to in excess of 100%. Once you got into debt with the gangster, you usually never totally paid off the debt.

This all sounds so much like what we hear everyday. And it is. The common bank or financial institution took note of the practices of gangsters and made those practices legal for the banks. The result is the credit cards of today, which are designed to lend money to people who do not normally qualify for typical financial institutional loans. The credit cards provide for extremely high interest loans. They have rates of 20% - 40% a year calculated monthly on the outstanding balance. They are designed to get you in debt and keep you in debt for the rest of your life. The greatest distinction of these credit cards is that they are legal, but this lending practice is not ethical. In fact, a good respectable bank that still makes loans at a few points above the prime rate will not offer that low-interest product if you go to them asking for money. Instead, they will tell you about a credit card you can get and use whenever you wish without any further application or review. While the credit card does not carry the name of the bank, rest assured, it is still a company owned by the bank. So the ethical bank will offer its customers a very unethical product and make a lot of money. And the best part is that it is still perfectly legal.

What a story. The banks of the world copied the practice of the gangsters of the world and got away with it. So today, gangsters no longer offer loan shark services; they were put out of business by the legal banks.

So how do you fix this mess? It is simple. Responsible government must step in and stop the practice before it destroys the poor and middle class. How? Why not use the same set of anti-racketeering laws that were used to stop the gangster years ago? Since the banks copied the practices of the gangster, then they are most likely easy to classify as violating the same laws that were finally used to stop the gangsters.

The second example considers a different industry. It is the insurance business. Now I am not talking about the insurance practices for whole life, term life, auto, medical, or home policies. Some of those practices are beginning to come into question too, but they are not my argument. Have you ever priced whole or term life insurance? It is very expensive insurance. Considering the pricing of whole and term life insurance, one has to wonder how the insurance companies can offer such low cost accidental life insurance polices. For about ten dollars a month you can get a $100,000 accidental life insurance policy. A regular whole or term life insurance policy for a value of $100,000 would cost $150 to $200 a month. So how can all the insurance companies offer such cheap accidental life insurance policies? And if that is not enough, you can get an accidental life insurance policy without a physical or even a requirement to respond to health questions. Why? Because the insurance companies do not plan to ever pay an accidental life insurance claim. For sure, there will be one or two exceptions to suggest that the policies are legal, but the majority of the claims will never be paid.

You can file a claim, but you will be surprised by things such as requiring a physical examination after a person's death and using the results as grounds for rejecting the claim. The wording of the policy, in just a very few paragraphs, is specifically designed to assure claims will never be paid. If you ever read such a policy, you will find it very hard to imagine a case that would qualify as an accident. Even lawyers will tell you it is nearly impossible to get an insurance company to pay a claim on an accidental life insurance policy. So you cannot get an attorney to aid you in processing a claim unless the amount of the claim is so excessive that the attorney will be able to negotiate with the insurance company and still make a significant percentage of profit. In most cases, that would take a class action case to make it worth the efforts required by the attorney.

All of the major insurance companies are offering these accidental life insurance policies. I think they got the idea from the gangsters. The gangsters use to call it protection. You pay him to protect you from other gangs. In reality you were paying him to protect you from him. A gangster was never expected to have to provide any kind of payoff or service for a claim against the protection insurance. That is why the amount you paid stayed small enough for you to continue justifying it as a necessity, large enough for him to stay in business, and small enough not to draw undue public push back. As long as everyone who would question the practice was also on the take, i.e. getting a share of the profits from the practice, there would never be any trouble. Now everyone is on the take with today's accidental life insurance policies. For example, did you notice most offers for accidental policies come via other institutions, such as your job, bank, auto insurance company, or credit card company? Well they are all paid a fee to present you with the offer. So they are essentially on the take too. The practice of accidental life insurance is legal, but very unethical.

So what can be done to fix the problem? Well some things do not yield themselves to clever solutions. This is one of those things. The practice just needs be made illegal. It is just that simple. Cancel your accidental life insurance policy, even if it was offered in your name by a bank at no cost to you. If everyone refuses the product, then it will disappear from being offered.

These are just two of several examples of unethical, but yet legal businesses.

Mule Sense 101 – If only one mule uniquely made you rich, then that mule was used unethically

A Fool's Knowledge

Mule Sense 101 Rules
Look at the birds. They don't plant, harvest, or gather the harvest into barns, yet they eat. If you leave a mule along, he will also eat

Mule Sense 101 (Fool's Knowledge)

So what is mule sense? Or what is a fool's knowledge? It really is simple and the concept has been around since the beginning of time.

W. Edwards Deming developed and wrote about a system of profound knowledge. It is a complete transformation of a company which facilitated the importation of new knowledge from outside the company. The system focuses on first changing the individual leaders and workers and finally ends with changing the processes by which we communicate and work with each other. The logic is simple, obtain knowledge that otherwise would never come forward in the operations of the business.

To some degree, Deming was ahead of his time in that he initiated concepts that are commonly implemented today. When you study the details of Deming's fourteen points of a system of profound knowledge, you will conclude most of the points are accomplished today under cultural diversity.

But the words coined by Deming are important. He called it profound knowledge. I called it mule sense or a fool's knowledge. I had no real reason for that tag, other than it was a funny response when someone asked me how I came up with such logical approaches to resolving issues. I used to simply tell them it was common mule sense, something everybody on the farm understood. They would laugh, but never question the knowledge, because it was never taught at Harvard Business

School or any other school. Some may even call it just plain common sense.

Early in my professional career, I used to be a Financial Management Trainee. The program I participated in was offered by a very famous company and had enough historical success that many considered it to be equal to an MBA. Without an accreditation, that claim of being equal to an MBA program may be hard to prove. But it was a great program and it offered many enriching experiences. One of those experiences clearly demonstrated the value of profound knowledge or mule sense, which I mentioned earlier in this book.

As part of my training, I had the opportunity to attend a meeting of a leadership team of one of the largest business segments of the company. These leaders were so far above my pay grade that I never accomplished the task of getting to their level in my entire career.

I was under the impression that leaders at this level analyzed an issue, considered all the possible solutions and selected the best solution. Then I assumed they applied all of their outstanding skills to make their collective solution work. Boy was I wrong. There were no skills expressed in that meeting. No one presented any concrete analysis or even solid potential solutions. Instead, these leaders sat around the table and discussed experiences they were having at home with their families and used the logic of those experiences as the basis of their major business decisions. I could not believe it. I sat there and wondered why I went to college and studied all I had learned. After all that effort and years of study, I found that those at the very top made decisions based on what I learned as a child on the farm. And even more importantly, they were not that good at using their experiences. I sat there and burned inside to tell them where they were misapplying their family knowledge. I was sitting in that room burning to speak profound knowledge or as I call it mule sense. What an eye opener. The best business judgments are nothing more than mule sense.

Over the years, that has not changed. Every now and then someone came up with a refreshing and seemingly new approach to doing business. Maybe it was a new process or even a new product. But when you pull back the layers and understand the new process or product, it is just common sense. Since it was applied in a way no one ever considered before, it therefore became mule sense or as Deming would call it, profound knowledge.

So that is what mule sense really is. This book is just a collection of a few mule sense ideas that are rumbling around in my head. It is just something out in left field that makes a little sense. There is more, but these things should always be taken a little at a time. Already there is more here in this document than

I have ever expressed at any single time or setting. If it makes your head swim, then just read a little at a time. Rest a day or two between readings.

I need to tell you one more fact about mule sense. Mule sense is not earthly natural thinking or wisdom. It involves a portion that is not of our earthly minds. I will not take you down the path of religion, but let me just say that the best way to achieve the outside view Deming discussed is to obtain it from someone outside this world. So if you get your mule sense from the One accredited with making this world, then your mule sense will be truly unique. My mule sense is the gift of the word of knowledge. It is not wisdom, which is how to use knowledge; it is just the knowledge.

Mule Sense 101: – Look at the birds. They don't plant, harvest, or gather the harvest into barns, yet they eat. If you leave a mule along, he will also eat.

Mule Sense 101 Rules
Don't waste the brains of workers
It is ok to let workers think
The customer is always right and so is the worker
Listen to your elders
Work if you want to eat
Never eliminate profit
Eliminating the customer eliminates the business
Don't use envy to set prices
Don't use assumptions to set higher prices
Don't set prices assuming Americans will pay anything
Base airline ticket prices on cost and not volume
Cheap airline tickets are not tickets for everyone to fly
Your phone still works!
Always keep the mule working
The mule is the valued asset and must come first
Houses are not mules. Houses are depreciable fixed assets
Don't buy a mule you cannot afford
Mules stay at home, they never walk off just to go visiting
If you take a mule across town and leave it, the mule will find its way home
A mule's life today is the same as it was 100 years ago
All advertisement does not work
You do not have to add advertising revenue to everything
Everybody does not like your ads
A tired mule blocks out orders and stops listening
If only one mule uniquely made you rich, then that mule was used unethically
Look at the birds. They don't plant, harvest, or gather the harvest into barns, yet they eat. If you leave a mule along, he will also eat

Another Book By

Darris L. Martin

I Come To Bring Living Water

I am the bearer of Living Water. I am come to bring Living Water. The grass of a field, the lily of a valley and people will dry up and die without water. How much more so will your soul perish without the Living Water of life. I am not the creator of the Living Water and I am not the Living Water. I am just the bearer of the Living Water. "But whosoever drinketh of the water that I shall give him shall never thirst: but the water that I shall give him shall be in him a well of water springing up into everlasting life." (John 4:14)

Available at:

www.lulu.com

www.darrissite.com

www.amazon.com

www.ebay.com

www.cheapesttextbooks.com

www.bookwire.com

www.barnesandnoble.com

And other great on line book stores.

Darris L. Martin

In the Body of Christ

Darris Martin completed Able Ministry training at Gospel Crusade, Incorporated (a non denominational religious retreat, bible school, missionary and church) in Bradenton, FL. Darris was ordained by the same church. While Darris is a fully ordained minister, he prefers to remain in his calling as a Bible teacher. Darris is also licensed as a Minister of the Gospel by Morning Star Baptist Church of Woodstown, NJ under the leadership of the Reverend Benjamin Mike, Pastor.

Mule Sense 101 (Fool's Knowledge)

In the Community

Darris Martin has been active in most communities he has resided. Over the years the two most significant involvements were managing a pilot temporary housing facility for displaced individuals under HUD in Daytona Beach, FL (these housing facilities are now available nation wide) and Treasurer of Homeland Charities, Incorporated. Homeland Charities is a U.S. 501-C3 non-profit organization that aims to alleviate the devastating impact of HIV/AIDS in Abia State, Nigeria. To meet this goal, Homeland has assembled collaborators, sponsors, endorsements, and resources that will provide comprehensive, innovative and cost-effective programs of Prevention, Treatment, and Research.

In the Work Place

Darris Martin is retired from Lockheed Martin after 37 years of service, where he last held the position of Electronics Systems Senior Quality Engineering Manager. He managed the

Mule Sense 101 (Fool's Knowledge)

implementation of several key corporate initiatives.

Darris has a Bachelors Degree from Indiana University in Business Finance. He resides in Pilesgrove, NJ.

Mule Sense 101 (Fool's Knowledge)

www.ingramcontent.com/pod-product-compliance
Lightning Source LLC
Chambersburg PA
CBHW032008190326
41520CB00007B/405